THIS BOOK BELONGS TO:

....

HIKING ACTIVITY BOOK for KIDS

35 FUN PROJECTS for YOUR NEXT OUTDOOR ADVENTURE

AMELIA MAYER

Illustrations by Cait Brennan

ROCKRIDGE
PRESS

For general information on our other products and services or to obtain technical support, please contact our Customer Care Department within the United States at (866) 744-2665, or outside the United States
at (510) 253-0500.

Rockridge Press publishes its books in a variety of electronic and print formats. Some content that appears in print may not be available in electronic books, and vice versa.

Interior and Cover Designer: Gabe Nansen
Art Producer: Hannah Dickerson
Editor: Julie Haverkate
Production Manager: Riley Hoffman
Production Editor: Melissa Edeburn

Illustrations © 2022 Cait Brennan
Borders and patterns courtesy of Shutterstock.com

Paperback ISBN: 978-1-63878-890-4 | eBook ISBN: 978-1-63878-541-5
R0

This book is dedicated to my little hiking crew and five adventure buddies. I love hiking with you most!

CONTENTS

Chapter 3—There's More to What You See: Touching, Smelling, and Listening 29

Chapter 4—You Can Be Creative: Making Art in Nature 49

continued >

LETTER TO CAREGIVERS

A s a mom of five very active children, I have become increasingly passionate about the outdoors and the benefits it provides not only to me and my kids but to *all* kids and adults. I've hosted an online outdoor family community for 10 years, and I can tell you that kids thrive in the simplicity of nature. They love doing hands-on activities with natural objects more than anything else.

Hiking is a fantastic way to spend time together, develop a great appreciation for the outdoors, and inspire kids' self-confidence. The activities in this book are meant to educate, encourage, and promote unplugged adventure.

I recommend starting this book with chapter 1; then, feel free to skip around. You'll notice that I have avoided being region specific and encourage both urban *and* rural exploration. So, go ahead and adapt the activities to your own situation.

Now, let's go hiking!

A Note on the Activities in This Book

Hiking and the great outdoors provide opportunities to be challenged, and both organically teach kids how strong and capable they are. Although kids should hike with an adult, those ages six to nine can initiate and complete most of the activities in this book by themselves. Activities 2, 13 to 16, 26, and 30 require some adult assistance and supervision. The icon below will identify such activities.

As they hike, kids will develop an intimacy with the world around them. My hope is that they will pass their learning on to others.

The Whys and Wheres of Hiking

Hiking is for everyone, but it's easier for some than others. Kids who can readily access mountain trails will have a different kind of experience from those hiking in urban environments. Kids with learning or mobility challenges may find hiking in any environment challenging. Opportunities for hiking may be comparatively limited for families lacking hiking gear or leisure time.

Here's the good news—there is increasing support for getting *everyone* out hiking. Check out the Resources for Caregivers on page 90 for affordable hiking gear, hiking programs, and transportation options.

You can do the activities in this book anywhere—in both urban and rural environments—whether you're technically hiking or not.

BE A HAPPY, HELPFUL, AND HONEST HIKING ADVENTURER

Hiking is not only great exercise (which makes you a happier kid) but it allows you to experience amazing views, terrains, and wildlife in a variety of geographic settings.

Hiking is also a big responsibility since future hikers depend on you to keep the trails in tip-top shape. As you do the activities in this book, you'll earn stars that make you an exceptional hiker *and* a budding naturalist. You should be proud that you're getting outside, exploring, and learning!

As a reminder, always go hiking with an adult you trust. Hiking with family and friends is also fun, so bring them along.

MY HIKING OATH

As a hiker, you're responsible for protecting the land you walk on and the nature and wildlife around you. Take this short oath and then sign your name at the bottom.

> I promise to teach others what I learn and to protect all hiking trails, nature, and the wildlife I see so that everyone can enjoy them for years to come.
>
> *Signed:* ....

Some DOs and DON'Ts When Hiking

Hiking comes with some important "dos" and "don'ts." You'll learn about some of these more in-depth in chapter 1, but this is a good place to start. Share these with other kids you're hiking with.

DO smell flowers, but DON'T pick them.

DO take photos, but DON'T damage anything or leave behind any trash.

DO sing on the trail, but DON'T make your own trail.

DO observe wildlife around you, but DON'T get too close.

DO pick up sticks or leaves on the ground, but DON'T pick up a bird's nest or an animal's home.

DO take deep breaths to smell nature around you, but DON'T put anything in your mouth (without asking an adult first).

What to Pack?
Preparing for Your Hike

Prepare your day-hiking bag, and you'll be ready to go anytime. Take a few minutes with your adult and gather the following materials. It's okay if you don't have all of these items right away.

- [ ] **This book and a pencil**
- [ ] **Blank journal**
- [ ] **Cell phone for communication and taking photos (or bring a camera)**
- [ ] **Compass**
- [ ] **First aid kit (See activity 2 on page 4 to build your own.)**
- [ ] **Jacket and hat**
- [ ] **Paracord (a lightweight nylon rope), string, or yarn**
- [ ] **Rain poncho or survival blanket**

Snacks (See activity 3 on page 6 for ideas.)

Sunscreen

Water bottle

Whistle

CHAPTER 1

GETTING READY TO HIKE

Hiking is one of the best all-inclusive outdoor activities because it can be done anywhere. In this chapter, you'll discover what hiking is and how to get started safely and responsibly.

You'll learn how to:

- Recognize what a hike is
- Build your own first aid kit
- Pack snacks that fuel your body
- Leave no trace
- Plan a hike

Activity 1: Defining a Hike

Have you ever wondered what the difference is between a hike and a walk? Test your knowledge below by answering whether an activity is a hike or not.

Activity	Is it a hike?	
▶ Exploring your backyard with your family?	YES	NO
▶ Walking around your neighborhood and looking at nature?	YES	NO
▶ Climbing rocks?	YES	NO
▶ Walking along boardwalks while taking in the sights?	YES	NO
▶ Climbing up stairways of tall city buildings to get a good view?	YES	NO

Believe it or not, the answer to all these questions is YES! If you're on an adventurous walk, you're hiking! You can hike on trails, on sidewalks, or on the beach. You can hike through a forest, a city, a park, or your own neighborhood.

Who Hauls All Your Gear?

Sometimes on longer hikes, you need to carry more food, water, and gear. The good news is that there are special animals that can help carry that extra weight. Llamas, goats, and horses are all great pack animals that can carry what you can't. They love hiking, too.

NOW YOU KNOW!
Great job! Now you know what hiking is so you're ready to get started!

Activity 2:
DIY First Aid Kit for Kids

Being prepared when going on a hike is a good idea in case an accident happens. Build a small first aid kit by gathering the following materials:

- ► 2 antiseptic wipes

- ► 5 bandages

- ► Gauze pad

- ► Pair of latex or vinyl gloves

- ► Small bottle of hand sanitizer

- ► Sandwich-size resealable plastic bag

- ► Roll of adhesive tape

- ► Small bundle of toilet paper

Fill the plastic bag with the materials. Remember, replace any used supplies when you get home.

How to Clean a Wound

If you or someone in your group gets cut while you're hiking, be sure to clean the wound right away.

1. Carefully wash the wound with clean water.

2. Wipe the wound with an antiseptic wipe and let it dry.

3. Cover the wound with a bandage so it stays clean.

NOW YOU KNOW!
Now you know how to make your own first aid kit to keep you safe when hiking. You did a great job!

Activity 3: Snacks—Making Your Own Trail Mix

Snacks are an important part of hiking. They give you energy you need to log miles, scale mountains, or just stay happy as you move your body. If you start to feel tired or grumpy, there's a good chance some food and water will give you the boost you need.

Trail mix is a great hiking snack. It's easy to pack and gives a quick boost of energy with protein, healthy fats, and a little sweetness, too.

Favorite Trail Mix Combos

Not sure what to include in your trail mix? Try one of the following:

Classic Mix: Candy-covered chocolates, peanuts, raisins, small pretzels

Energy Mix: Almonds, cocoa nibs, yogurt-covered raisins, dried cranberries, pumpkin seeds

Tropical Mix: Cashews, coconut flakes, dried mango pieces, banana chips

NOW YOU KNOW!

Now you know what to pack to give your body fuel to keep hiking. You're going to have some really yummy snacks!

Activity 4: Leave No Trace

"Leave No Trace" is a saying people use to respect the land and wildlife when hiking. Try these activities:

How close is too close to wildlife?: Cover one eye, and stick your thumb up and your arm out straight. Try to cover the animal with your thumb. Still see it? You're too close! Back up and try again.

Pack it in, pack it out: Don't leave anything behind. Any trash you bring, even a banana peel, needs to be taken with you.

Trash Breakdown

Did you know it takes years for trash to break down? A piece of fishing line can take 600 years to decompose. When possible, reuse or recycle materials you take on your hike, like a reusable water bottle.

NOW YOU KNOW!
Now you know how to "Leave No Trace" and why doing so is important. The wildlife will thank you!

Activity 5: Planning Your Hike

Before you go hiking, research your trail using local guides and maps. Write the answers to these questions in your hiking journal so you can remember them when you're on the hike.

▶ How long is the trail?

▶ How much time do you need for the hike?

▶ What is the elevation change of the trail?

▶ Is there shade?

▶ Is there anything neat you should watch for (waterfalls, caves, petroglyphs [rock art], lakes, etc.)?

Map Key

When you're looking at a map, find the map key with symbols that represent important features or places on a map.

NOW 𝒴OU KNOW!
Now you know what to look out for on your hike. Way to be prepared!

CHAPTER 2

TAKE A CLOSER LOOK:
Observing, Tracking, and Identifying

It's easy to miss amazing things when you're hiking. The activities in this chapter help you slow down, listen quietly, and take a closer look at nature.

You'll learn how to:

▷ **Observe nature in more detail**

▷ **Identify types of trees**

▷ **Follow a trail**

▷ **Identify animal tracks to learn about wildlife**

▷ **Practice orienteering**

Activity 6:
Nature Scavenger Hunt

- -

With so much happening all around you, a scavenger hunt is a great way to open your eyes a little wider and see what you can find in nature.

For this hiking scavenger hunt, copy what's in the squares on the next page in your journal or write directly in your book. As you hike, check off items you see. Can you spot them all before you end your hike? If not, bring your scavenger hunt items with you next time. You can do this together as a group or individually.

Make Your Own Scavenger Hunt Card

Want to keep going with this activity? Make your own scavenger hunt card. Draw the items or list them like in the squares on the next page. Laminate your card or attach it to a clipboard to carry as you hike for easy reference.

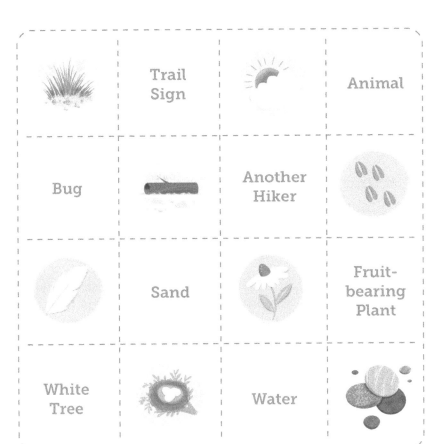

	Trail Sign		Animal
Bug		Another Hiker	
	Sand		Fruit-bearing Plant
White Tree		Water	

NOW YOU KNOW!

You did an awesome job observing nature with your eyes! Keep going and practicing for even more fun!

Activity 7: Tree Huggers

There are two main types of trees: deciduous and coniferous. Deciduous trees, like maple, oak, and birch, have broad leaves that change color and drop in the fall, and these trees spread their seeds with flowers. Coniferous trees, like Douglas fir and lodgepole pine, have needles, and cones spread their seeds.

To play the game, decide who will be the "Tree Master." As you hike, the Tree Master calls out the kind of tree (example: "Deciduous!"). Everyone runs to hug a deciduous tree. The last one to hug the right kind of tree is "out."

Keep playing until only one person is left. That person is the new Tree Master.

When the Trees Are Scarce

Sometimes you'll be hiking where there are no or few trees. Don't worry! The "Tree Master" can call out other items, like types of rocks, bushes, or grasses native to the area.

Coniferous

Deciduous

NOW YOU KNOW!
Now you know how to identify different types of trees as you hike. Bonus: Impress others by using the words "deciduous" and "coniferous"!

17

Activity 8: Trail Signs

Many different kinds of signs are used to mark trails. As you hike, look carefully for these different signs. Draw the first one you spot so you can remember it and count how many you see during the hike.

Sign post: Gives the name of the trail and sometimes provides an arrow showing which way the trail goes

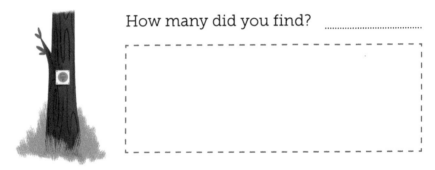

How many did you find? ....

Trail blazes: Usually bright spots of paint on trees along the trail

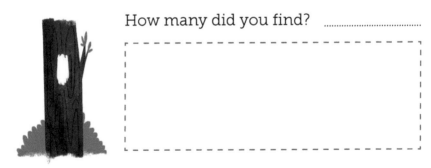

How many did you find? ....

Cairns: Piles of rocks to show where the trail goes

How many did you find? ....

History of Hiking

The concept of hiking is a relatively new one. By the late 19th century, as more and more big cities were built, people wanted to spend more time in nature for recreation. "Outing clubs" became popular in the United States and Europe to promote outdoor activities, like hiking.

NOW YOU KNOW!
Now you know how to spot trail markers so you're sure you're following the right trail as you hike!

Activity 9: Identifying Tracks

Animals are everywhere, and the easiest way to identify what animals have been where is by looking at their footprints or tracks. This activity is easier when tracks show up clearly, like in sand, mud, or snow.

Look around and see where you can find tracks. Think about the feet that make the tracks. Are they small or big? Heavy animals, like deer or moose, will make deeper tracks, whereas lighter animals, like birds or lizards, will leave shallower tracks.

Decide on how you want to measure the tracks you discover. You can use your hands, feet, or a stick you find to measure. Record your measurements and sketch the tracks you see in your hiking log (see page 26). See if you can guess what animal made them.

Movement Clues

If you look closely at animal tracks, you can even tell *what* animals were doing. For example, look where the animal's toes are pointing to see what direction they were going. Do you think the animal is hopping or flying and landing? Look for tracks that stop and start again.

NOW YOU KNOW!

Now you know how to identify animal tracks—and even what the animal was doing. Keep watching for tracks as you hike!

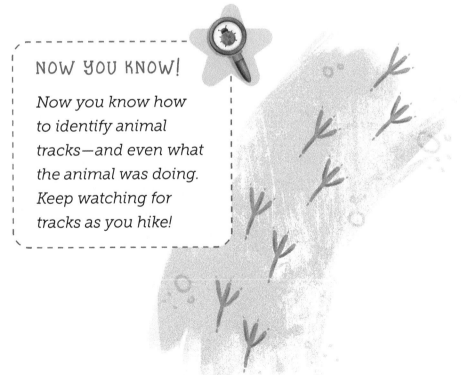

Activity 10: Looking Ahead

Remember to look ahead while hiking. This game can help you observe nature as you go.

Take turns playing this game as you hike. Start by looking ahead on the trail and picking out something you see. Tell your friends and family what color it is. Let them ask questions about the item that you can answer only with a "yes" or "no." Time is up when you can't see the item anymore.

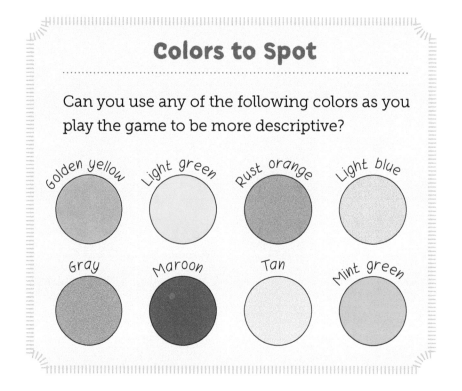

Colors to Spot

Can you use any of the following colors as you play the game to be more descriptive?

Golden yellow   Light green   Rust orange   Light blue

Gray   Maroon   Tan   Mint green

Activity 11: Orienteering Treasure Hunt

In this activity you will practice your observational orienteering skills, or how to create and follow a map.

1. Hide an object like a water bottle near the trail.

2. Write instructions on how to find the object without saying where it is. Example: "Hike 20 steps toward the big rock and then turn right."

3. Give the instructions to a family member or friend to follow. Did they find the object? If not, try again! Rewrite until they can find what you hid.

Use a Compass

A compass always points north in case you get turned around. Use the saying "**N**ever **E**at **S**oggy **W**affles" to remember the cardinal directions of north, east, south, and west.

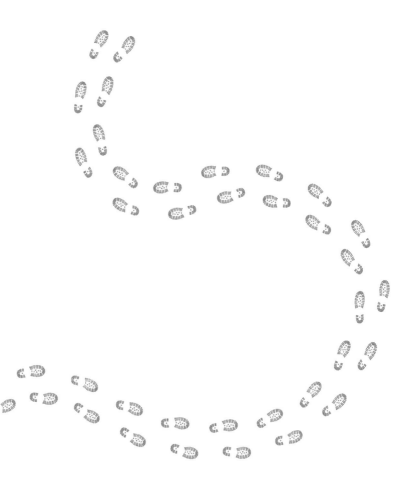

Hiking Log

Keeping a log is a helpful way to remember your hikes. Need more room? Use your journal.

What do you remember about your hike? *Was it hard or easy? What did you notice (wildlife, sign posts, sounds, etc.)?*

Sketch what you saw on your hike. You can paint or draw an interesting scene or an animal you spotted.

CHAPTER 3

THERE'S MORE TO WHAT YOU SEE:

Touching, Smelling, and Listening

Experience nature with your five senses. This chapter guides you to see, smell, taste, hear, and touch as you hike.

You'll learn how to:

▸ Listen carefully to the sounds of nature

▸ Identify what's safe to touch and what's not

▸ Focus on the smells of nature

▸ Look closely at your surroundings

▸ Identify different plants

▸ Make music with nature

▸ Compare different seeds

Activity 12: Sound Hunt

Did you hear that? Is it the sound of chirping birds, a babbling brook, rustling leaves, or something else? You can hear nature all around you.

1. Talk with your family or friends about what kinds of sounds you might hear on your hike (scurrying animals, howling wind, people talking, etc.).

2. Stand or sit still for 30 seconds and just listen. Closing your eyes can be helpful.

3. Staying quiet, make a list of the sounds you hear and if you can tell what is making them. Can you hear at least 10 different sounds?

4. Gather with your group and see if, together, you found 50 different sounds or more.

5. Do this every time you hike. Are the sounds the same or different? If in a city, can you tell the difference between nature and city sounds?

Imitate the Sounds

This activity can be even more fun if you try to re-create the sounds yourself. What sound effects can you make? Practice bird calls, the sound of wind, or even the sound you hear animals make. Can you get your friends and family to guess what sound you're imitating?

NOW YOU KNOW!
Now you know how to listen more carefully to the sounds of nature. Your ears will thank you!

Activity 13:
Sensory Exploration

- -

Nature is *full* of different types of
textures! You can examine things
that are safe to touch while you enjoy
your hike.

1. Start by looking for small items (pieces of bark,
   small rocks, leaves, flowers, etc.) as you hike.
   Ask an adult if they are safe to touch before
   examining them.

2. Close your eyes and touch each item, discovering
   the different textures. How do they feel? Smooth?
   Rough? Bumpy? Damp? Soft? Squishy? Hard?

3. Remember: Leave No Trace! Once you've finished
   your sensory exploration, return each item to the
   spot where you found it.

Leaves of Three, Let It Be!

Beware: There are some plants in the wild that you really *don't* want to touch! They are poisonous and can give you an awful rash. One of the most common is poison ivy, which grows in sets of three leaves. For other examples of plants to avoid, look at the pictures:

Poison Ivy

Poison Oak

Stinging Nettle

Giant Hogweed

Poison Sumac

Activity 14:
Nose to the Ground

- -

Nature has a lot of different smells.
Take a few minutes to turn off
your other senses so you can really
experience nature through your nose.

1. Close your eyes. Ask an adult to watch so you don't bump into anything.

2. Get as low to the ground as you can. What do you smell? Carefully move around and see if you smell different items as you explore with your nose. Can you identify different trees or plants?

3. Slowly move higher and smell as you go. Are the higher-up smells different from or the same as ground-level smells? Be sure to record them in your hiking log (see page 46).

Smelling Nature Is Good for You

Did you know that taking some big whiffs of nature's smells can reduce stress? Try to identify your favorite smells on your hike. Do you smell flowers? Pine boughs? Salty sea air? Fallen leaves? How does each make you feel? Take some time to do some deep-breath smelling as you hike.

NOW YOU KNOW!

Now you know how to focus on the smells of nature. Some will be pleasing to your nose (like flowers) and others may be offensive (like decomposing leaves!).

Activity 15: Looking Closely

Sometimes it's easy to miss the small, but great, things all around you as you hike. Take the time to stop and look closer while you walk.

1. Grab a camera and go a little ahead of the hiking group to take a very close-up photo of one part of an object along the trail. If you don't have a camera, draw a very small part of an object. Make sure you don't go too far ahead. You want an adult to always be able to see you.

2. Show the photo or drawing to everyone in your group.

3. Give everyone a defined area to search for the object in the image. Who can figure out first what the object is?

Identify Flower Parts

Find a flower and take a photo of the very middle of it. Can you identify the flower's parts by matching them to the diagram here? You'll probably have to look very closely. Sketch the flower parts in your hiking log (see page 46).

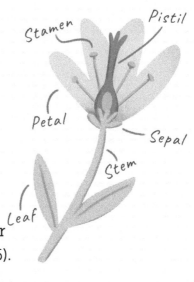

Stamen

Pistil

Petal

Sepal

Stem

Leaf

NOW YOU KNOW!

Now you know how to look really closely at nature. You can even identify different parts of a flower—what a great skill!

Activity 16: Nature's Snack

You can find edible berries in nature during the right season, but you need to know what you're looking for. Always ask an adult before you taste anything.

1. Before you set off, do some research as to what berries you may see on your hike. Berries are usually ripe in the late summer, but the time depends on the amount of rain and temperatures that year.

2. Collect berries and enjoy eating them as you go. Be sure to watch out for other animals who may also be enjoying the berries.

3. If you manage to collect enough berries to be able to bring some home, they are amazing on ice cream or sprinkled on oatmeal. If you're really patient, collect enough to bake a pie.

Berry Good

The berries you may find vary widely depending on where you are but here are some to look for: blackberries, cloudberries, elderberries, huckleberries, and gooseberries.

NOW YOU KNOW!

Now you know how to look for snacks on the trail. And you've gotten some experience in identifying more plants—great work!

Activity 17: Making Music

Listening to nature is important, but joining in with the sounds by making your own music can be really fun. Remember to enjoy yourself, but don't be so loud that you scare any wildlife.

Look for items in nature you could use to make some music. Sticks of different sizes work great for drumsticks. Use rocks or sticks to slide across objects with different textures to make sliding sounds. If you're around water, make some splashing sounds.

Sound Off!

▷ Most animals use sounds to help them detect dangers and hazards.

▷ Flies cannot hear any kind of sound at all. Not even their own buzzing.

NOW YOU KNOW!
Now you know how to join in with the sounds of nature. What beautiful music!

Activity 18: Looking to the Sky

The clouds in the sky can tell us a lot about the weather. Big and fluffy clouds mean good weather ahead, but dark, puffy clouds could signal that snow or rain is coming.

Take a break to sit and look at the clouds. What do they tell you about your hike? Do you see any pictures in the clouds? Take turns pointing out fun shapes or wacky characters. Can you tell a story from the clouds?

Why Are Clouds White?

They are made of water droplets and ice crystals that scatter all light, making them appear white.

Activity 19: Seed Sorting

Plants make more plants by spreading seeds. You can find seeds all over in nature, looking for their next place to grow.

Take a hike through some tall grasses and see what sticks to your shoes, socks, and clothes. Remove the seeds and save them. Now that you have your seeds, sort them by size, color, and shape. Which is the biggest? Which kind is the smallest?

Seed Spreader!

Seeds can be found in flower heads, tree cones, and berries. Winds can spread seeds far away, allowing new plants to grow in surprising places!

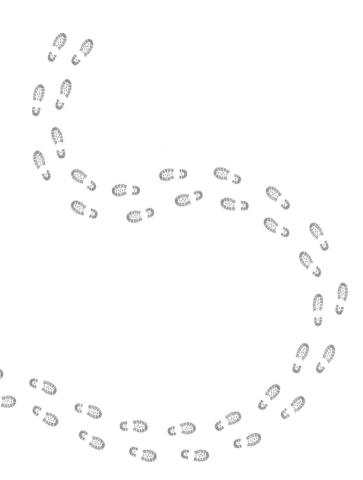

Hiking Log

Keeping a log is a helpful way to remember your hikes. Need more room? Use your journal.

What do you remember about your hike? *Was it hard or easy? What did you notice (wildlife, sign posts, sounds, etc.)?*

Sketch what you saw on your hike. *You can paint or draw an interesting scene or an animal you spotted.*

CHAPTER 4

YOU CAN BE CREATIVE:

Making Art in Nature

Creating art with natural objects is a fun break from hiking! All of these projects use items you already have with you or that you can find in nature.

You'll learn how to:

▶ **Create a picture on the ground**

▶ **Paint with water**

▶ **Make a magical hiking stick to help you on your hike**

▶ **Follow the tradition of fairy houses**

▶ **Make art and structures using only natural materials**

▶ **Imitate historical art forms**

Activity 20: Natural Picture Building

The time to get creative on your hike is here! Take a break and look around for materials you can use to build a picture on the ground. Berries, flowers, grasses, leaves, pine needles, rocks, seeds, and sticks all make great materials. Don't worry about what you're going to make—this activity is about using your creativity to turn natural items into a beautiful work of art. Gather what you can hold for now. You can always go back for more.

Take your materials and find a flat spot to create. You may choose a tree stump, the top of a boulder, or a flat piece of land. Can you make a person? A landscape? An animal? Be creative!

Be Inspired!

Check out the artist Andy Goldsworthy for some amazing sculptures made entirely out of items from nature. Take photos of your art like he does and then be sure to return your items back to where you found them to follow the "Leave No Trace" principle.

NOW YOU KNOW!

Now you know how to use natural materials wherever you are and build beautiful pictures. Keep those creative juices flowing!

Activity 21: Water Painting

Water makes everything more beautiful! For this activity, use a natural water source or, if needed, water from your water bottle.

1. Start by looking for a water source such as a stream, ocean, dew on leaves, a puddle, or your own water.

2. Gather items to use as a paintbrush such as pieces of moss, a wad of grass, a leaf, or even a long, sturdy palm leaf.

3. Dip your different "paintbrushes" in the water and paint on natural items around you. Notice how each "paintbrush" makes different patterns.

4. Practice painting different strokes or write your name. Notice the colors that appear as you paint. Record this in your hiking log (see page 66).

Just Add Mud

Ready to take your water painting a step further? Mix dirt and water to make mud. Use your different "brushes" to paint with the mud on rocks or trees. Looking for more color? Try crushing berries or flowers to see what colors you can make to paint with.

NOW YOU KNOW!
Now you know how to make more art using only what nature provides—and you know how to mix your own paint. Nice work!

Activity 22: "Magic" Hiking Stick

Nature is magical on its own in its stillness and beauty, but a "magic" hiking stick adds to the fun and just makes hiking easier.

1. Find a large stick and gather materials such as feathers, moss, leaves, or small branches to add to the stick.

2. Take your cord or string from your backpack and carefully tie it on one end of your stick.

3. Wrap the cord around the stick as you secure the natural items you found. Keep wrapping until you are out of cord and all your items are attached to your stick. Tie a knot to secure the cord.

4. Use your magic hiking stick to get you down the trail. If you'd like, keep adding on more treasures you find along the way.

Remember the Journey

The items you collect for your magic hiking stick will help you remember your hikes. The next time you head out on a hike, bring more cord and add even more items. Bring your stick with you whenever you hike, and use it to help share your hiking adventures with others when you get home.

NOW YOU KNOW!
Now you know how to make a magic hiking stick that will help you down the trail. Have fun with it!

Activity 23: Fairy House

It's so fun to build houses for fairies or small animals and imagine who will visit them. Remember to only use natural materials so you're not leaving any trash behind, and keep the fairy house to the side of the trail.

1. Think about what your fairy house should look like. Will your creation be short and wide, or tall and skinny? Will you make the house on the ground or in a bush?

2. Find a flat rock or piece of bark for a base. Use materials like wood, bark, or more rocks to make walls. Your roof can be made with the same materials or try out vines, branches, or leaves.

3. Be sure to make a door so fairies or small animals can visit. You may also want to make a welcoming walkway that leads to the door.

Fairy Villages

Fairy villages are a long-standing tradition in the woods of many places. From the Isle of Man in the Irish Sea to the coast of Maine in the United States, fairy villages are a favorite tourist attraction. See if you can find one near where you live. You never know where they might pop up.

NOW YOU KNOW!
Now you can build your own magical fairy houses and continue this fun tradition. Keep up that creativity—you're doing great!

Activity 24: Mud Stew

"Cooking" mud stew is a super messy, super fun way to take what you find in nature and make something (almost) yummy. Leave the tasting to the animals, though.

1. Find a concave-shaped (curved and hollow) rock, a hollow tree stump, or a hole you dig in the ground to make your stew.

2. Look for items you would like to mix into your stew. Berries, flowers, grass, leaves, tiny rocks, and sand are all good ingredients.

3. If you have water, add it to your stew. If not, just mix everything together with a stick.

4. Serve your stew in bowls made from anything you can find on the trail like large leaves or empty shells. Doesn't your dish look delicious?

Muddy Mud Stew Recipe

Ingredients

- 3 cups mud or sand

- Water, as needed

- 2 cups torn-up leaves

- Pinch of pine needles or grass

- 1 handful seeds

Directions

1. Mix the mud with the water until soupy.

2. Stir in the leaves and pine needles.

3. Top with the seeds.

4. Serve.

NOW YOU KNOW!

Now you know how to use only natural items to make something creative and fun. Have fun experimenting!

Activity 25: Nature Maze

Building a maze is a fun way to challenge your creativity. Sticks or grasses work great, but you can use any materials you find.

1. First draw your maze in the sand or dirt using a stick.

2. Build your maze by outlining the path you drew with natural materials. Start in the middle and work your way out in a circle or square shape. You may have to redo your design as you go.

3. Follow the maze!

Put It Away

When you're done with your maze, be sure to take it apart and put the sticks back where you found them. You don't want other hikers tripping.

NOW YOU KNOW!

Now you know another way to be creative in nature and practice following a path!

Activity 26: Nature Weaving

Weaving is an age-old skill that is fun to do in the middle of summer when you can use soft and flexible grasses.

1. Ask an adult to help tie four sticks together to make a square by binding their corners with cord or string.

2. Use another piece of cord to go back and forth to make lines about 1-inch apart across the square.

3. Weave items you find, like grasses, over and under the cord.

Weaving throughout History

Weaving baskets is one of the oldest crafts humans have mastered. Not only are weavings beautiful, they can help haul food and water, too.

Activity 27: Rock Towers

For centuries, people have been building rock towers called cairns to help mark trails. Let's build rock tower sculptures *off the trail* just for fun.

1. Find a place with lots of rocks. A riverbed or a rocky beach are great for rock stacking.

2. Starting with larger rocks on the bottom, build towers that gradually end with small rocks on the top.

3. Before you leave, sketch your towers in your hiking log (see page 66) and put the rocks back where you found them.

Stop the Erosion

Moving rocks on trails can cause erosion (a breakdown of the land because the rocks are no longer holding up earth). Build cairns only in areas where there are already lots of rocks.

NOW YOU KNOW!
Now you can carefully and responsibly build rock towers, a skill you could use if you were ever blazing a new trail!

Hiking Log

Keeping a log is a helpful way to remember your hikes. Need more room? Use your journal.

What do you remember about your hike? *Was it hard or easy? What did you notice (wildlife, sign posts, sounds, etc.)?*

Sketch what you saw on your hike. *You can paint or draw an interesting scene or an animal you spotted.*

CHAPTER 5

LAUGH AND LEARN:
Having Fun and Playing Games

These activities are a fun way to make hikes or hard trails just a little easier.

You'll learn how to:

▶ **Search for specific aspects of nature**

▶ **Create games using only natural materials**

▶ **Challenge your memory on the trail**

▶ **Take turns leading a hike**

▶ **Change the way you walk**

Activity 28:
Hiking the Rainbow

- -

Let's go on a colorful adventure! This game will bring you on a rainbow-colored treasure hunt as you search for items of different colors on the trail.

1. As a group, review the colors of the rainbow so everyone is clear on the order: Red, Orange, Yellow, Green, Blue, Purple.

2. Begin with looking for something red together as a group. When you find a red object, say "RED!" out loud.

3. Continue on through each color of the rainbow until you have found and hiked the whole rainbow. Depending on where you're hiking, this could take a few minutes or the whole hike. See the next page for examples of objects to look for.

4. If you get through the rainbow quickly, replay the game but with different objects, or focus on different shades of a particular color. Try challenging yourselves to only hunt for colors you find in nature (rather than a car or backpack, for example).

Red cardinal   Orange poppies   Yellow
                                    blooming cactus

Green   Blue rock   Purple
sagebrush   huckleberries

Colors for Safety

Always wear bright colors when you're hiking
so you can be seen easily. Wearing highly
visible clothing ensures you won't be mistaken
for an animal during hunting season!

NOW YOU KNOW!
*Now you know how to search nature
for the colors of the rainbow. You did great!*

Activity 29:
Nature Tic-Tac-Toe

You can make a game out of anything you find in nature, whether you make up the game or play one you already know, like tic-tac-toe.

1. In the ground, mark out a 3-by-3 grid with a stick or rock.

2. Ask everyone to look for six matching game pieces for each to use for the game. Some ideas of what to look for are rocks of the same color, acorns, fallen flower petals, sticks of the same size, etc.

3. The first one back to the grid after finding their pieces gets to go first.

4. Take turns placing your pieces down and trying to get three in a row, either diagonally, horizontally, or vertically.

Don't forget to clear the trail of your game and Leave No Trace!

Game Extensions

For even more fun, change out your pieces every round you play. Race to find new matching pieces and get back to the grid first. The winner of each round can choose where the other must search for their next pieces.

NOW YOU KNOW!
Now you can set up and play a game like tic-tac-toe using only natural materials. Congrats—you're doing great at hiking games!

Activity 30:
Roving Hide-and-Seek

You can play games that help you practice being quiet and listening carefully. For this one, be sure to always stay close to the trail and not get *too* far ahead.

1. Take turns running a little ahead on the trail to hide. The rest of the group stays behind and counts to 25 with their eyes closed.

2. Stay within about 10 feet of the trail and hide behind rocks, trees, or other easily accessible places. Stay quiet and use the time to listen to nature.

3. If the group passes you on the trail and no one has found you yet, yell, "I love hiking!" and catch up.

4. If they didn't find you, you get to hide again.

5. Take turns being the hiders and the seekers.

Stationary Hide-and-Seek

If your adults are nervous about you playing roving hide-and-seek, try playing the game in one stationary spot instead. As a group, set boundaries so everyone knows where they can and can't go. Get creative! Hide while lying flat in grasses, safely climbing up trees, or tucking behind boulders.

NOW YOU KNOW!

Now you know a fun way to practice being quiet and listening. You also know how to play more games in nature! Fantastic work!

Activity 31: Trail ABCs

Play this ABC game as you hike down the trail and see if you can get to "Z" by the end of your hike. Finishing is harder than you think!

1. Look for an object you see on your hike that starts with an "A." This object could be found in nature or something you see around you, including on other hikers. For example, you could look for an acorn, airplane, or animal.

2. Once you find an object that starts with "A," move on to "B," then "C," and so on until you get through the whole alphabet. Can you get to "Z" before you head home?

3. Too easy? Try looking for items only found in nature.

Trail Spelling

For an added challenge, try spelling words instead of looking for ABCs. For example, spell T-R-A-I-L and look for items that start with a "T," "R," "A," "I," and "L." Other examples of words you can spell are H-I-K-I-N-G, N-A-T-U-R-E, or your names.

NOW YOU KNOW!
Now you know a new way to explore nature. Keep up the excellent work!

Activity 32:
Nature Memory Challenge

- -

This game is a fun one to play while you are taking a snack break. Have one person start the game by finding 10 to 20 small objects in secret. The items should be natural like pine cones, rocks, seashells, sticks, etc.

The game leader arranges the objects on the ground and covers them with their hat, jacket, or another item. Then the rest of the group is given a 10-second peek at the objects before the cover is put back over the objects. The goal of the game is to try to name as many objects as possible from that 10-second peek. How many can you name?

Memory Champ

Unless you're hiking near the ocean, you probably won't see any dolphins. But did you know that these animals have the longest memory of any species except for people?

NOW YOU KNOW!

Now you know how to challenge your memory on the trail. The more you practice, the better you'll get!

Activity 33:
Leader Change-up

Being the leader of a hike can be really fun. This game is all about taking turns while listening super carefully to nature.

Choose a sound you hear often as you hike. Depending on where you are, this could be a bird chirping, a child singing, or leaves rustling.

Every time you hear that particular sound, the person leading runs to the back of the line and a new person becomes the leader of the hike.

The Words You Say . . .

Another way to play this game is to change positions every time someone in your group says a certain word (like "hike," "tired," or "hot").

NOW YOU KNOW!

Now you know how to have fun taking turns leading a hike. You're a great leader—keep it up!

Activity 34: Wild Animal Walk

The time has arrived to get a little wild! When you're feeling unmotivated, change up the way you walk.

Begin by choosing different walks for everyone to imitate as you move down the trail. Consider the animals you might see as you hike like a wild rabbit, snake, or mouse. No animals around? Move like a rolling rock, the blowing wind, or waves crashing on a beach. Take turns choosing and following the leader.

Why Animals Move

The way animals move is essential to their survival. Animals have to move to find food, to look for a good place to live, or to escape predators.

NOW YOU KNOW!

Now you know how to change up your walk, whether you want to waddle, hop, or run. Have fun being silly—and keep moving!

Activity 35: Following My Footsteps

This game is particularly fun in muddy or snowy trail conditions, but sand also works great.

1. Take turns being the leader and making footprints in the trail with your shoes. These can be regular hiking steps or silly ones.

2. The hikers behind you need to follow *exactly* in your footsteps.

3. Sing a song together as you step. When the song is over, the next person takes the lead.

Songs to Sing

Not sure what to sing? Here are some fun tunes everyone should know:

▶ *The Ants Go Marching*

▶ *Row, Row, Row Your Boat*

▶ *Old MacDonald* (in your version, use animals you might see on your hike)

NOW YOU KNOW!

Now you know how to be just as good a follower as a leader. Keep practicing those skills to become an even-better hiker!

Hiking Log

Keeping a log is a helpful way to remember your hikes. Need more room? Use your journal.

What do you remember about your hike? *Was it hard or easy? What did you notice (wildlife, sign posts, sounds, etc.)?*

Sketch what you saw on your hike. You can paint or draw an interesting scene or an animal you spotted.

CONGRATULATIONS!

Finishing these activities and going on hikes has officially earned you the title of **Hiking Adventurer**! You know how to find your way down the trail, keep yourself and your fellow hikers safe, and more carefully observe the outdoor world. You also know the *joy* of hiking as you laughed through some really fun games and discovered new ways of enjoying nature. That's what hiking is all about! The skills you have documented in your hiking logs (see pages 26, 46, 66, and 86) and journal are ones you can refer back to often as you share your adventures and skills with those you love. Happy hiking!

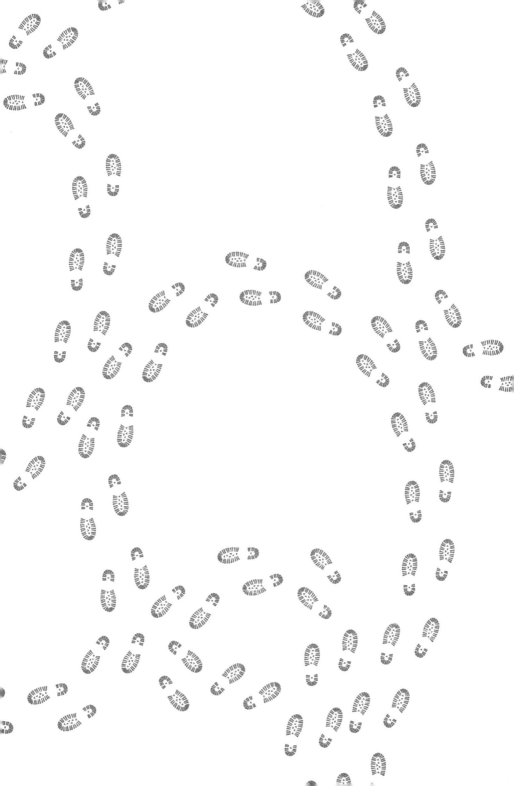

RESOURCES FOR CAREGIVERS

The following websites and books will advance your child's hiking skills.

OTHER RESOURCES BY THIS AUTHOR

🍃 **Camping Activity Book for Kids: 35 Fun Projects for Your Next Outdoor Adventure** by Amelia Mayer

If you're ready to take your outdoor trips with your hiking adventurers to the next level, try camping! This book by yours truly will help kids tackle survival challenges, learn how to tie knots, make a sundial, and more.

🍃 **Tales of a Mountain Mama** TalesOfAMountainMama.com

This is my self-plug for my site where we constantly publish new articles to help families get hiking and enjoying the natural world. Find tips, updated gear recommendations, and recommended trails around the country. Check out free guides for each season to help get your family and friends out in nature and hiking, biking, and enjoying outdoor challenges.

ADDITIONAL RESOURCES

🍃 **AllTrails**
AllTrails.com

With over 200,000 searchable trails, this app includes trail info, maps, reviews, and photographs and is a great resource for finding good trails in your area at the challenge level you and your family are seeking.

🍃 **Awesome Outdoor Science Experiments for Kids: 50+ STEAM Projects and Why They Work** by Megan Olivia Hall

If, on the trail, your kids ask questions like "What makes plants grow?" and "Why do bears hibernate in the winter?" this is the book for you. The included experiments allow kids to interact with nature and the amazing processes that occur all around them.

⌇ **Exploring Nature Activity Book for Kids: 50 Creative Projects to Spark Curiosity in the Outdoors**
by Kim Andrews

If your young hikers crave even more creative projects in the great outdoors, look no further! This book includes 50 outdoor projects that can be done anywhere and will inspire curiosity and interactive play as kids observe animals, plants, and even outer space.

⌇ **Hike It Baby**
HikeItBaby.com

This website isn't *just* for hiking with babies—it's a great resource for getting hiking with kids when you're first beginning and is also a fantastic place to find other hiking families.

⌇ **Local Trail Guide Books**
Want to plan your hike in advance? Check out your library or local bookstore for the best trail guides for your area. Whereas many trail guides can be found online, they are generally not as dependable as printed guides. Don't worry,

though, if you can't get your hands on these printed versions—many trailheads will have guides available to take with you.

🖊 **Outdoor Family Chat**
Facebook.com/groups/OutdoorFamilyChat

An online community group is a great place to ask questions and get support. This one is a good place to start, but there are many, so find the one that works best for you, your little hikers, and the natural area you're looking to explore.

ABOUT THE AUTHOR

Amelia Mayer grew up hiking the mountains of Alaska as a child motivated by chocolate and strawberries. She now loves hiking with her own husband and five children in the mountains of Wyoming. Because of her own hiking struggles as a child, she has a passion for instilling a love of hiking in kids from a young age. She works to provide a supportive community at TalesOfAMountainMama .com with tips and tricks, inspiration, gear reviews, and seasonal guides.

ABOUT THE ILLUSTRATOR

Cait Brennan is an easily excited illustrator. Her work celebrates peaceful moments in nature, kids and kids at heart, travel, and adventures of all sizes. Her favorite projects are ones that transport you into another world where your imagination roams free. In addition to drawing a lot, Cait loves making big messes in the kitchen and exploring dusty antique shops.

Printed in the USA
CPSIA information can be obtained
at www.ICGtesting.com
LVHW021456160524
780487LV00007B/20